To Alison
Blessings!
Simon

RIᵥERLUTION

Going with the flow of personal & planetary change

Simenon Honoré

Published by

Spirit of the Rainbow™

If you would like to contact Simenon Honoré please write to:

Spirit of the Rainbow
P. O. Box 483
Tunbridge Wells
TN2 9QU
United Kingdom

You can also find Simenon Honoré on **YouTube** and **Facebook**
Or visit our website at: www.spiritoftherainbow.org
Printed and bound by CPI Group (UK) Ltd, Croydon, CR0 4YY

ISBN 978-0-9566767-4-0

© Simenon Honoré 2015

OTHER BOOKS FROM THIS AUTHOR

- **WE ARE ONE** *A Manifesto for Humanity*

- **FINDING JESUS OURSELVES** *A Path of Spiritual Empowerment*

- **THE COMMUNITY OF CHRIST**

- **WELCOME TO PLANET EARTH** *A Guide For Awakening Souls*

To Peter Goldman

For The Illuminated Journey

☼

ACKNOWLEDGEMENTS

A special thanks to Patrick Houser and Niki Honoré for their work in helping with the preparation of this text and not least for their valuable spiritual insights.

☼

NOTE TO THE READER

The ideas in this book are the fruits of a lifetime's work seeking answers to questions about life. They aim to provide *an* answer not necessarily *the* answer. Readers must decide for themselves which ideas they want to work with and can adapt them to suit their own needs.

In this book I have mentioned authors that I have found helpful in illuminating the issues I have explored. If you are interested, further details are given in the footnotes. I have found them all valuable in some way though I do not necessarily share all their views.

☼

NOTE ON DATES

In this book I have used 'BCE' (Before the Common Era) and 'CE' (Common Era) to indicate dating, rather than the specifically Christian 'BC' and 'AD'.

CONTENTS

PREFACE

The idea for this book sprang from a conversation I had with the Complementary Therapist Bridget Mary-Clare in 2001. I can't remember what we were talking about but she used the word in a specific context:

"Not revolution but riverlution"

Where the conversation went after that is anyone's guess. Bridget used the word once, with meaning but in passing. In my squirrel-like way, I stored it away, thinking it sounded interesting and had potential. By temperament I like to mull things over, sometimes for years, even decades at a time till in my oddly ordered way I feel it has found its proper place in the universe (or possibly my universe).

What I found was that it gave a name to something I could sense but until then could not find a word for. What was more it covered a wide range of fields from the planetary to the personal and so it gradually took shape as a coherent theme that stretched literally right across the universe. And so 'riverlution' was born.

INTRODUCTION

Riverlution

There is a river that runs through life. And if we follow its course it will take us to our highest destiny. It is a river whose beauty lies beyond our imagination for it glistens and sparkles as it reflects the sunlight of our soul.

We can see this river in many ways: as our natural evolution, our path of the Spirit or God's plan for us. Sometimes it will be as a gentle brook. Other times the current will run fast and deep or we can find ourselves becalmed in its stillness, for this river flows at its own pace. It is neither forced nor delayed. But it will always flow with a Divine purpose.

Following the river is an act of faith. The more we are prepared to let go and trust, the more it can silently yet powerfully guide our lives: for we will never know quite what lies just beyond the bend, where the river will take us, how it will flow. This is the challenge that the river presents us with and its essential quality. It asks us not to know, not to be in command but to accept the mystery. It asks us for our trust with the promise that we may touch eternity. And so we reach our point of surrender. This is when we let the Spirit in. This is our leap into the light.

As the river begins to flow through our lives we feel its power refreshing us. We begin to awaken to its spirit and experience the freedom that it brings. We sense we are being carried along a higher pathway, no longer at the mercy of events but able to flow through them. We do not flee from challenges but rather are able to experience them more fully, embrace them, learn from them and then let them go. We realise that we no longer need to struggle. Fear gradually falls away from us. We do not need to be in control anymore. Yet in no sense are we passive. Our lives are intense and active yet at the same time at our soul level effortless.

The course of the river can take our lives in quite unexpected directions and for this we need to be prepared to be open to all kinds of new experiences. Ultimately it means being willing to enter into the unknown. And that kind of willingness does not necessarily come easily.

This is particularly true if we live in a culture that puts its faith in working out a plan for life arrived at by 'rational' (i.e. intellectual) decision making. Career strategies and maps for living can be useful tools to begin our life's journey with. But there comes a point where if we are get any further we have to abandon our plans, throw the map away, let go and put our trust in the flow of the river. This is when the Spirit can really begin to work through us and shine freely in our lives.

There is a paradox in our act of surrender to the power of the Spirit for it is this that really sets us free. Allowing ourselves to be carried along by the force of an invisible river may seem like an act of abdication of our responsibilities or just sheer madness.

But the point to understand is that it is *our* river, part of our soul, part of who we really are. We are moving to a higher state of consciousness.

My personal struggle has been - and continues to be - to reach that point when I surrender to its flow. This does not always come easily for me, for low self-worth tells me to be driven in all I do, fear that I must always be in control. To live and let go surely has been the greatest challenge for me and the journey never ends. Yet through all the twists and turns of my life, this issue has always faced me. Words inspired by Jesus[1] call to me over and over again:

"BECOME LIKE A CHILD AND TRUST"

The hesitant steps I have taken have meant the greatest liberation in my life: to finally lay down my burden and melt into the flow of the universe.

---

[1] Mark 10:14 "Let the little children come to me, and do not hinder them, for the kingdom of God belongs to such as these." (*Holy Bible*, New International Version, Hodder & Stoughton, 2011)

The universe itself follows its own riverlution. We can see it in the evolution of the cosmos with all its varied elements and life forms. Whether we define its dynamics as the Laws of Evolution or God or some quite other subtle mechanism at work is neither here nor there. What is important is gaining the sense of its flow. This is a river that flows through the entire universe and it is flowing through us right now.

Riverlution also manifests as a natural creative impulse that courses through everything from the Milky Way to microbes. It's the same impulse that makes humans want to paint or have children. Irresistibly powerful, riverlution can operate in the gentlest and most delicate of ways as a butterfly drawing nectar but also as the force behind the giant Nebula explosions that can rip galaxies apart.

Nor is it to be supposed that it always follows a smooth and even flow. The pattern of evolution indicates moments of relatively steady development interrupted by intense spurts of evolutionary growth. Cataclysmic events can destroy millions of species only for life to reassert itself in different forms.

In human development, riverlution seems to feel its way: various species and sub-species take root in different parts of the world. *Homo sapiens* has now emerged, carrying within it elements of other species including Neanderthals. Is this process over? No, riverlution is an eternal process.

OUR FREE WILL

Riverlution is an inevitable and irresistible force in the universe. So where is our free will in all this? The question of free will can be understood at many different levels but in the sense that it applies to the flow of the universe we can look at it in various ways.

The first is to see it as a sailor would: that the tides, winds and currents are part of nature over which she or he has no control but the task is to learn to navigate them successfully. Within this image lies an important spiritual truth: to sense when the wind is flowing in our favour and to unfurl our inner sails; to know when the tide is turning and leave the safety of the harbour to set out on our adventure. It could be a process of self discovery, a pilgrimage, an inner spiritual journey or a walkabout in the wilderness. It's about going with the flow – creatively and purposefully.

The great spiritual teacher Omraam Mikhaël Aïvanhov described the role of free will as having a universal script already written in which we 'audition' for various parts: to take the story of Jesus, someone 'won' the part of Peter and someone else got Judas' role as a result of the choices they made in life, past and present.

So we could say the story of the universe is set but our roles in it are not.

To tweak this idea we could say that though the broad sweep of the play is already written, there is some room for 'improvisation' by the actors: through our motives and actions we can change the outcome at least of various Acts, if not the entire play. And then there is the question of the ending. Here too we can add a twist to the plot:

1. EVERYONE ESCAPES IN THE FINAL REEL!
2. THERE IS NO FINAL REEL...

Equally we can see each of us with a canvas on which we create our own individual painting, our unique 'take' on the universe. We are free to paint any picture we like but we will inevitably paint it. And in the end, all our paintings are beautiful.

The flow of this invisible river affects us not only as individuals but as nations too for each country has its own destiny to follow. The planet on which we live follows its own riverlutionary course as does the universe itself. How we manage it, how we tune into it, and learn to follow its course, is the subject of this book.

So I invite you to turn the page and discover more of its wonderful magic.

CHAPTER I

Universal Riverlution

There is a flow in the evolution of our universe that will guide our ultimate destiny. It operates within each of our lives and determines the fate of the stars. Flowing from its source, it evolves and explores all the possibilities of its existence; and then it returns to its origin. Such a cycle may be repeated many times in many different ways. It is as true of a flower as of the human soul and the cosmos itself. And it is inevitable.

When we look at the evolution of the universe, the easiest way to understand principle behind the process is to see the way our lungs expand and contract as we breathe in and out. Most scientists believe that at the moment of its creation the entire universe was concentrated into a single incredibly dense point called the 'singularity'. The universe - space, matter, time - expanded from this point and has been doing so ever since. This is the 'Big Bang Theory'. [2]

It is worth pausing a moment on the 'Big Bang Theory' whose roots extend as far back as the Middle Ages and

---

[2] According some scientists, it is better to think of the Big Bang as the simultaneous appearance of space everywhere in the universe; as space itself has been stretching, it has carried matter with it.

encompass not only science but religion and art. Charles Darwin's grandfather published a poem[3] over 200 years ago in which these lines are said to foretell the ideas behind 'Big Bang':

> *"'—LET THERE BE LIGHT!' proclaim'd the*
> *ALMIGHTY LORD,*
> *Astonish'd Chaos heard the potent word;—*
> *Through all his realms the kindling Ether runs,*
> *And the mass starts into a million suns;*
> *Earths round each sun with quick explosions burst,*
> *And second planets issue from the first;*
> *Bend, as they journey with projectile force,*
> *In bright ellipses their reluctant course;*
> *Orbs wheel in orbs, round centres centres roll,*
> *And form, self-balanced, one revolving Whole.*
> *—Onward they move amid their bright abode,*
> *Space without bound, THE BOSOM OF*
> *THEIR GOD!"*

Erasmus Darwin's poem was not based on scientific observation: it was intuitive. Yet the story of scientific discovery is entwined with that of intuitive insights. What Einstein called "a leap in consciousness" has taken humanity forward in its understanding of the universe. Later scientific evidence provides the proof.

---

[3] Erasmus Darwin, *The Botanic Garden,: a poem, in two parts* (London, printed for J. Johnson, 1791)

Riverlution itself is at heart an intuitive sense which history has illuminated.

Darwin's poem also illustrates a theme that runs through our story of the universe: the interaction between the two great orthodoxies, religion and science. The fact that he saw a vision of evolution that went beyond the traditional literal view of the creation story in Genesis yet still saw God as the initiator of the evolutionary process was to dog the controversy over the Big Bang Theory.

The modern scientific idea of a 'Big Bang' to explain the origin of the universe was based on the work of Georges Lemaître – who was both a priest and physicist. Using Einstein's equations of general relativity, Lemaître established in 1927 that the universe itself was in motion, either expanding or contracting. Even Einstein at first was sceptical but the astronomical observations of Edwin Hubble two years later confirmed that galaxies were rushing away from us: in other words, the universe was expanding. And, as Lemaître pointed out, if it was expanding now the further back in time we went the smaller it must have been. So at its birth, logic suggested it would have been concentrated in one single incredibly dense point. It was from this that the 'Big Bang Theory' was born.

The theory at first aroused a storm of controversy. Big Bang described what happened after the moment of singularity but it didn't describe why it happened, where it came from or what was there before it. It therefore opened itself to the possibility of a supernatural origin to the universe as seen in Darwin's poem. Supporters of 'Big Bang' like George Gamow were accused of being closet Creationists and the announcement by Pope Pius XII that it was consistent with Christian teaching may have strengthened the suspicion. No doubt the role of Georges Lemaître as a priest fed into this narrative.

Its leading opponent, Fred Hoyle, found the idea of Big Bang that allowed for the possibility of a Creator, to be "pseudoscience", explaining, "For it's an irrational process, and can't be described in scientific terms."[4] In a BBC interview, Hoyle said, "The reason why scientists like the 'Big Bang' is because they are overshadowed by the Book of Genesis. It is deep within the psyche of most scientists to believe in the first page of Genesis."[5] Or perhaps the memory.

That it was eventually accepted, mainly by observations carried out by Hubble and others,

---

[4] Quentin Smith, A Big Bang Cosmological Argument For God's Nonexistence (*Faith and Philosophy.*, Volume 9, No. 2, April 1992)

[5] Adam Curtis, "A Mile or Two off Yarmouth" (BBC, 24 February 2012)

illustrates the interaction between what can be at first intuitively sensed and later what science can establish.

Now scientists accept that at the moment the universe is flowing outwards a new question has emerged: how will the universe end? If we follow the analogy of the lung we see how eventually the universe will reach the limit of its expansion and begin to contract till its reaches its starting point – the singularity. This theory – called 'Big Crunch' – has its supporters in the scientific community; some believe further that the cycle of expansion and contraction would start all over again.

Yet even this scientific theory was also preceded by the work of imaginative and intuitive authors. Foremost amongst these was a 'Prose-Poem' by Edgar Allen Poe, better known for his horror stories. In his work *Eureka*,[6] Poe set out his vision of the evolution of the universe:

"My general proposition, then, is this:- In the Original Unity of the First Thing lies the Secondary Cause of All Things, with the Germ of their Inevitable Annihilation."

He went on to describe in considerable detail – explaining that he was drawing both on science and intuition – how from a "primordial Particle" matter spread out till there was an inevitable reaction, the

---

[6] Edgar Allen Poe *Eureka* (George Putnam, New York, 1848)

universe would draw back into itself and reach the moment, "when the bright stars become blended - into One".

Poe's story did not end there. For he echoed not only the 'Big Crunch Theory' but the cyclical model where the process repeats itself:

"A novel Universe swelling into existence, and then subsiding into nothingness, at every throb of the Heart Divine."

Edgar Allen Poe's lengthy work was not well received. Some thought it was a joke. He must have sensed its likely reception because in his Preface he wrote:

"To the few who love me and whom I love - to those who feel rather than to those who think - to the dreamers and those who put faith in dreams as in the only realities - I offer this Book of Truths, not in its character of Truth-Teller, but for the Beauty that abounds in its Truth; constituting it true...

What I here propound is true: - therefore it cannot die: - or if by any means it be now trodden down so that it die, it will 'rise again to the Life Everlasting'."

Yet Poe's central idea of a universe that expands and contracts is now part of the currency of modern science.

The current main rival to Big Crunch – 'Big Freeze' – sees a cold, dark and empty universe that has run out of energy to create new stars and planets. For now this is a matter of speculation and debate in the scientific world as the Big Bang Theory once was.

THE UNIVERSAL FLOW OF GOOD AND EVIL

The flow outwards from a point of origin, the sense of reaching its fullest extent before it flows back to the source, applies to the journey of the soul as to the universe. From a Universal Soul or Creator, each soul evolves and explores through a series of life experiences, adding its own distinctive colour to the sum of universal understanding and awareness.

We can see the path the soul takes as a spiral: descending from the subtle levels of existence to experience the denser regions that are planetary life; returning to the higher planes at the time of death, the soul takes with it all the knowledge it has gained during its time on earth; and once it has reflected on it, it begins a new life of learning on earth.

Eventually all souls will have fulfilled the potential of their exploration in this universe and return to the Source, that primordial Light at the heart of all universes that some call God. Perhaps in another universe another series of explorations will begin and the process of expansion and contraction will continue in another form or in parallel.

This flow of our soul's evolution can shed light on the question of good and evil: whatever encourages and supports us in our soul's evolution is helpful and good. Similarly, whatever holds us back, whatever keeps us from our growth or even seeks to take us backwards is harmful or evil.

We see this link with Dr Martin Luther King who sought to take America forward in its evolution and fulfil the promise of its original vision of equality, life, liberty and happiness that are to be found in their Declaration of Independence - the spiritual source of the United States of America.[7]

Dr Martin Luther King has earned his place in history as a great civil rights leader but he gave even more to humanity through his insights:

"Darkness cannot drive out darkness: only light can do that. Hate cannot drive out hate: only love can do that."[8]

---

[7] See Simenon Honoré *The Eternal Ark of the Covenant* (Spirit of the Rainbow 2017)

[8] Martin Luther King Jnr *A Testament of Hope* (HarperCollins, San Francisco, 1991)

We see how he goes beyond the conventional thinking that if someone hurts you, you hurt them back. Instead we can respond from a place further ahead in our evolution, from a place of goodness. He once said to civil rights marchers that if someone hits them, respond not with violence but with a question:

"What kind of human being are you?"

Hitler in contrast sought to take Germany back to a primeval past. Nazism glorified race, hierarchy and territory, harking back to an ancestral animal world in its most savage form. He defined his own 'species' of 'predators' - the Aryans - and aimed to pit them against all others, destroying anyone he considered 'weak' or 'alien' in his twisted version of 'survival of the fittest'.

What the Nazis did was infinitely worse than any animal, which acts only out of instinct: humans have a choice. Hitler sought to awaken an ancient, dark power within his people and harness modern technology to commit industrialised mass murder.

Yet because the evolutionary flow of the universe is always towards the Source - that is, ultimate goodness - it means that good and evil are not equal forces. We can see this if we throw a paper plane in the wind: if we throw it in the same direction as the wind, it will fly a good distance; throw it against the wind it will not travel far and probably just blow back in our face. That is why the force of good is always more powerful than the force of evil.

This is important to understand because we live in a world where it often seems evil triumphs, which it certainly can do in the short term; over the centuries humans have developed a dualistic mindset where good and evil represent the two great forces locked in eternal and equal struggle. Even amongst people of faith, God, despite being God, seems apparently unable to do anything to ensure a victory for the forces of good. We need to understand that the flow of evolution - that is, the flow of good - is irresistible. A castle in the sand, however formidable-looking, can only resist the tide for so long. Riverlution shows the inevitability of the triumph of good over evil.

Riverlution also sheds light on how our sense of what is helpful or harmful, what takes us forward or holds us back, can change over time. If we see ourselves as travelling towards a spiritual sun, everything in front of us is in the light; behind us, everything is in shadow. As we are evolving, what falls within the light or darkness changes: as we take a step forward – that is progress; then we take a second step – more progress; but now the first step is behind us. If we tried to return to the first step, we would be regressing – even though when we first made it, it was progress!

So what was once a step forward can over time become not merely no longer helpful but even harmful: thus what is helpful or harmful, good or evil, can be a question of where they stand relative to each other in humanity's progress. We see this in ancient laws written for humanity at a time of tribal feuding and bloodshed. In the Code of Hammurabi and the Law of Moses, we find:

"An eye for an eye, a tooth for a tooth."[9]

Nowadays this can been seen as an encouragement to vengeance but at the time its intention may well have been to limit blood feuds so it should be read in the sense of *'only* one eye for one eye'. Some sources suggest we can also see it as paving the way for compensation – that is the *value* of an eye or a tooth should be paid for its loss. This is particularly significant because humanity is moving towards restorative justice and away from punishment (which is little more than legalised vengeance). So the sense of balance, which we find in the Torah, the book of Jewish Law, has emerged in a new way as we seek to make good the damage caused by criminal behaviour.

---

[9] Leviticus 24:20 (עין תחת עין, ayin tachat ayin)

23

This in turn leads us to a greater awareness of the difference between spiritual laws – such as justice, compassion and truth – which are for all time, and human laws, which need to evolve over time. In turn this leads the issue of Divine Law as it may (or may not) be expressed in sacred texts. If we suppose that every dot and comma of a Holy Scripture was dictated word perfect by God, not only does in fly in the face of all academic research[10], it confuses spiritual and human law: that which was written for the world in which the messenger lived, and that which was written for all time. It may be this that St Paul had in mind when he said:

"The letter kills, but the Spirit gives life." [11]

The Spirit of God, of universal evolution takes us forward to our highest destiny. The letter - the unchanging rigid letter of the law - can hold us back and just seem cruel and repressive to generations that have moved on.

---

[10] Even with the Qur'an, some Islamic scholars question whether all of it was written down at one period and suggest there may have been additions up to 150 years later. My feeling is that we can get an accurate sense of the Prophet's message from his Last Sermon, 632 A.C., 9th day of Dhul al Hijjah, 10 A.H. in the Uranah valley of Mount Arafat.
[11] Paul 2 Corinthians 3:6 (*Holy Bible*, New International Version, Hodder & Stoughton, 2011)

CHAPTER II

Riverlution In Our Lives

The sense of riverlution is with us from the moment of our birth if not before. We see this within the Islamic tradition: the idea that every child is born a Moslem. In Hadith 2:441 Abu Huraira tells us:

> *"Allah's Apostle said,*
> *'Every child is born with a true faith of Islam'"*

What does this signify? First, we must understand what the word 'Islam' means: submission - submission to the Will of God. So every child is born with this innate tendency to seek to do God's Will – to choose the highest path in following our spiritual evolution and one day to return to the Source. It is as if all humans were born with a homing device inside them.

So much of human longing, of creativity over the centuries - especially in art and music - can be seen as memories of 'Paradise Lost' or a search for heaven on earth. Somewhere inside us, we know from where we came. Somewhere inside us, there is a longing to return.

Riverlution then gives a sense of where we came from and where we are going. What about the journey itself?

Riverlution means that our personal and spiritual development can go at its own pace, neither forced nor held back. The spiritual teacher Peter Goldman used the phrase:

"Not before time nor ahead of time but in time."

Riverlution means that body, mind and soul work together in a natural rhythm. That means taking time to listen within so we can take *all* of ourselves along with us. This is important because in our enthusiasm and ambition we can run ahead of ourselves and lose our sense of natural flow.

Even – perhaps especially - in pursuit of the highest ideals – we can fall into the trap of ignoring our physical or emotional needs; or our expectations can be based on an inflexible timescale. We can end up trying to force ourselves to develop at an unnatural pace and by working in extremes we can make ourselves both emotionally and physically unwell.

Equally riverlution could mean becoming more active; that we stop procrastinating and commit fully to what we know in our hearts we are called to do.

To avoid the pitfalls of becoming driven or dragging our feet we can learn to listen to the flow of riverlution.

LISTENING TO THE FLOW

Listening to our intuition is the key to staying in touch with the natural flow of our lives. Intuition is a great spiritual gift to humanity. It enables us to feel into the underlying currents and eddies of life and sense what is right for us in any given moment. Intuition is a way through which our soul may speak to us. And for us to listen we need to learn to be still.

Stillness is something that people can be frightened of: sitting still, silence, the stilling of our thoughts and emotions – all these can instil genuine fear especially in industrialised societies where people have thrown themselves into a workaholic frenzy and made their madness a virtue. But it is in stillness we can reconnect with our own natural rhythms and tune into the pace and direction our souls seek to take. Our intuition will always guide us to our highest destiny if we let it.

During the course of our spiritual evolution, there will be times when we will be outgoing and creative; other times when we need just to be still and quiet; there will be times of steady growth and times of dramatic upheaval. Learning to go with the changing flow is all part of the process of fine-tuning our spiritual antennae.

Where we can be absolutely sure is in knowing that our willingness holds the key. As long as we are willing to follow our spiritual river, our highest destiny awaits us.

A VOYAGE OF RIVERLUTION

Every life is different and riverlution will not mean the same thing for all of us. Adjusting to the natural flow of our lives may be a gradual process or a dramatic one. Nevertheless drawing on my own life experiences, people may see elements that could be of use to them. The events I describe began in 2000.

A day came when my life made a decision to live in its natural flow. The decision was made for me when a hitherto unknown little elastic band inside me that was stretched beyond endurance went 'snap' and I started to fall apart. I could have tried to patch myself up and go back to the life I had before but something inside me told me this was my chance and I began to change my life as my life began to change. It took nearly ten years in all and a lot of adventure and I went through many difficult times as did those around me.

Eventually a new life emerged creating opportunities for me. First, I gave myself the space to be silent: it can be a few minutes meditation in the morning but I need it to nurture my soul; I also created times and places where I could be quiet; for me it is very important to be in nature so I can reconnect with a sense of the rhythms of the earth as I walk in the woods. Even the sight of a garden brings a joyful sense of the spirit of nature.

This in turn freed me to listen to the 'child within' that can intuitively sense our path of riverlution; then to take on work that had the potential to be interesting, important and joyful; to work the hours I needed to and also put aside time for my home and relaxation. Above all to embrace how precious each moment was. Gradually I found a simple joy and clarity in my life as I focused on the essential – the essence. And what is this essence? Our soul will tell each one of us...if we listen.

For now, I leave it to my diary, seven years after I began my search for a new life:[12]

<u>*August 12th 2007*</u>

> I have at last found work where I can do things properly, with love and care, with honour and integrity. It is a key piece of the jigsaw, a Simenon-shaped niche on this planet where I can earn a living to the joy of my soul. It provides a secure foundation on which I can build the rest of my life...Now I bear witness to the words of Jesus, words I know to be true - not as a matter of

---

[12] See Simenon Honoré *Walking With Jesus* (Spirit of the Rainbow, 2017)

dogma or even of faith, but because I have lived through them:

"Therefore I tell you, do not be anxious about your life, what you shall eat or what you shall drink, nor about your body, what you shall put on. Is not life more than food, and the body more than clothing? Look at the birds of the air: they neither sow nor reap nor gather into barns, and yet your heavenly Father feeds them. Are you not of more value than they? And which of you by being anxious can add one cubit to his span of life? And why are you anxious about clothing? Consider the lilies of the field, how they grow; they neither toil nor spin; yet I tell you, even Solomon in all his glory was not arrayed like one of these. But if God so clothes the grass of the field, which today is alive and tomorrow is thrown into the oven, will he not much more clothe you, O you of little faith? Therefore do not be anxious, saying, 'What shall we eat?' or 'What shall we drink' or 'What shall we wear?' For the Gentiles seek all these things; and your heavenly Father knows that you need them all. But seek first His Kingdom and His Righteousness, and all these things shall be yours as well."[13]

Two thousand years ago Jesus spelt out very clearly how to live and he has not been alone in delivering this spiritual message. What he says is very challenging – for us personally and the whole of society. It means

---

[13] Matthew 6:25-34

putting our trust in our highest destiny and going with the flow of our lives.

LIVING AND WORKING IN THE FLOW

Living and working in the flow means we accept our responsibilities, we do the work we need to each day, and we do everything differently because we are going with the flow of our evolution.

Following our universal flow intuitively in our daily lives means we seek to give ourselves the space to put thought and care into all we do, though there may be times where we need to work intensely and trust in our intuition to guide us. We listen inside for when we need to be still, even if for a few moments; we sense when it is right to forge ahead or when we have reached our limit. We are willing to explore and challenge ourselves and go further than we had imagined possible; and we know when to nurture ourselves.

In recent years I have done three very different kinds of work: teaching, writing and working in a warehouse. Each one responds to the flow of riverlution.

Writing is the simplest. I can easily fall into the twin traps of becoming driven or dragging my feet so I begin with a meditation and check into my inner sense of flow at intervals. I also balance the mental intensity of writing with physical activity like walking in the woods or working in a warehouse.

Working in a warehouse has its own structures: turning up at a specific time, working agreed hours, getting targets met. I work for different companies, most of which allow me and the other workers to set a pace that we can maintain throughout the shift. Regular breaks allow for an ebb and flow in energy and having flexibility in the way we work allows for changes in concentration and physical effort.

I did work – once – for a company that drove its workforce manically: everyone was stressed and angry, goods were thrown around the warehouse floor, workers' welfare, health and safety were disregarded in a mad dash for maximum production. Dangerous and stupid, it led inevitably to many mistakes being made and everything took a lot longer than it needed to. Worse, people were sacrificing their health and well-being for a nameless god that would never care for them however frantically they worked.

Teaching involves taking into account the changes in energy levels and focus of a group of people and so intuition is an invaluable tool. I needed to be willing to change the course and pace of the lesson at a moment's notice. I usually had several possible lessons in my head simultaneously so I could switch easily; or sometimes it was something a student said or did that provided the on-the-spot inspiration.

My own energy level needed to stay constant, which meant paying attention that I was getting enough sleep and what I was eating and drinking before lessons. Teachers are notoriously overloaded with work so I took the decision only to work part-time and sense when I had reached my limit and listen to it.

THE CHALLENGE OF RIVERLUTION

Following the course of riverlution is not a soft option and I have found it at times very difficult. The sense of flow brings an inner joy but the process of trying to turn my life Godways up can create turmoil within and without. For me it has sometimes a case of being dragged kicking and screaming towards my highest destiny!

I am also very aware how much I can still resist its flow. I can lose my connection with its eternal truth and become stressed and fearful and angry, forgetting the inevitability of goodness. Yet I have always that sense of universal flow to return to and relax into, surrendering my worries to the care of the Great River.

As we become more in harmony with the Divine plan for our lives we may find ourselves less in harmony with the prevailing drift of society and that may include people we know and care for. They may choose a different path and we may feel the loss though in truth we always remain connected in invisible yet important ways. As we progress we help take the world with us. Yet others will come into our lives who have listened to the call of our universal soul and we can join together in working towards our highest destiny both for ourselves and our society.

This means standing aside from a world that convinces itself that we must produce more, do more, say more and all at ever increasing speeds. People allow themselves to be helpless victims, sucked into in a whirl of frenetic activity imagining they must 'achieve', 'win', 'succeed' to be somebody. Rushing through life, we risk missing all our precious moments. Going with the flow of life we see its value.

For me the sense of its powerful presence has become more and more alive over the years and I have found a new life living simply and well. There has been a natural falling away of people and things that no longer support my soul's evolution. I have a clear focus in my life and an inner peace that comes with a sense of inevitable flow towards our Source.

CHAPTER III

A People's Riverlution

Riverlution applies not only to the great sweep of the universe and to our own daily lives but to nations too, for each country has its own destiny to follow. To find its natural course, a nation needs to listen within, listen to the different parts of itself, just as we need to do as human beings. And it must follow its highest path.

Where there is an open and effective dialogue between citizens and their government it is easier to find the right pace and direction for the country's evolution. There will always be individuals either in government or amongst the general public that may take the lead and encourage or inspire the rest of us to go further. Others will want to go more slowly, even try to turn the clock back. Just as there are eddies and cross currents in any waterway, this creative tension is part of the natural process of growth and change.

The task of government and society is to keep it within the boundaries of the great river's course through mutual respect and understanding. These are the banks that contain the river and stop it from flooding and causing damage. It means that riverlution can take place peacefully and constructively.

Riverlution is not, however, simply a question of finding a consensus around which everyone feels comfortable and that challenges no one. The unity we seek is not uniformity but the unity between society and its highest purpose. New ideas can be very unpopular to start with but that does not make them wrong. We need always to listen to that 'still small voice of God' even if there are those who would drown it out with the noisy prejudices of a conformist majority.

What we always need to do, however, is to understand and address the fears and worries of those whose initial reaction maybe to resist change so we create the best opportunities for people to move forward. The rest is up to them. This is where a government that is sensitive to the consciousness of a nation is so important. It needs to work not only towards the highest ideals but also taking into account where people actually are in their development.

However history has shown us many examples where governments are not responsive to the needs of the people. This is most likely to happen in dictatorships but democracies can be guilty of it too. It can occur in two ways: first, when the regime obstructs the legitimate aspirations of the people. It is as if a dam is created that blocks the natural flow of a people's development. Eventually the dam will burst with cataclysmic consequences. Second, when the regime goes too far ahead of its people and drags an unwilling populace behind. In one case the government is moving too slowly, in the other too fast. In both cases they are out of step with the natural flow of the nation's riverlution.

In 20th century Russia we can see both processes at work. The autocratic government of Tsar Nicholas II, last of the Romanov dynasty, ruled Russia at the beginning of the 20th century without a parliament or a free press and with little regard for human rights or concern for the welfare of its largely peasant population. New forces were beginning to stir in Russia - industrialisation, calls for reform and democracy - but the Tsar seemed unable or unwilling to embrace these changes.

Rather he sought refuge in the centuries old repression of his police state and his view of himself as "Father of his people". Indeed his stated and sincere belief was that God had given him a sacred responsibility to maintain his absolute authority and pass it on intact to his son. The fact that his family owed its position as rulers of Russia to political manoeuvrings 300 years previously seems to have passed Nicholas II by. No doubt he relied on the Church's traditional view that, in the words of St. Paul, "The powers that be are ordained of God", which rather conveniently meant him.

Consequently, when he was forced to concede the beginnings of a democracy following the attempted revolution of 1905, he saw it not as an act of enlightened statesmanship but as a betrayal of his God-given duty made in a regrettable moment of weakness. He thus spent the remainder of his reign trying to claw back the rights he had granted and so made it increasingly difficult for Russia to follow the path of gradual reform. In hindering the natural path of riverlution, The Tsar set up both himself and his country for a catastrophe.

THE DAM BURSTS

The First World War destabilised the Tsar's regime further as military defeats and the increasingly desperate plight of the civilian population exposed the failings of the regime. In February 1917 as riots over bread shortages threatened the government's control of the capital, the army was brought out on to the streets to crush the popular uprising. Here we see the moment when the forces of change overwhelm the forces of reaction and the dam finally bursts:

"...the tips of the bayonets were touching the breast of the first row of demonstrators. Behind could be heard the singing of revolutionary songs, in front there was confusion. Women, with tears in their eyes, were crying to the soldiers, 'Comrades, take way your

bayonets, join us!' The soldiers were moved. They threw swift glances at their own comrades. The next moment one bayonet is slowly raised, is slowly lifted above the shoulders of the approaching demonstrators. There is thunderous applause. The triumphant crowd greeted their brother clothed in the grey cloaks of the soldiery. The soldiers mixed freely with the demonstrators."[14]

In a desperate attempt to save the regime, members of the Russian elite persuaded Tsar Nicholas to abdicate. There followed a six-month window of opportunity for the forces of democratic change to set Russia on a new course. But the new Provisional Government was too weak and too tied to the past and the moment passed.

This politically bankrupt government was then overthrown in a second revolution that brought the Bolsheviks to power. Led by Lenin, the new communist regime more than matched their Tsarist predecessors in authoritarianism and ruthlessness.

Lenin's successor, Stalin, embarked on a course of rapid industrialisation and drastic agricultural reform. Millions of people died as the plans were carried out at break-neck speed in a frantic rush to meet virtually impossible targets with scant regard for the human

---

[14] *Illustrated History of The Russian Revolution* (Martin Lawrence Ltd, London, 1928). Quoted in Lionel Kochan *Russia In Revolution* (Paladin, UK, 1971)

cost. In effect the government was seeking to force the pace of change, way ahead of what the country and its people were capable of, resorting to the most appalling brutality to achieve its goals. Stalin's own words give us an insight into the driving force behind this behaviour:

"It is sometimes asked whether it is not possible to slow down the tempo somewhat, to put a check on the movement. No, comrades, it is not possible! The tempo must not be reduced! On the contrary, we must increase it as much as is within our powers and possibilities. This is dictated to us by our obligations to the workers and peasants of the USSR. This is dictated to us by our obligations to the working class of the whole world. To slacken the tempo would mean falling behind. And those who fall behind get beaten. But we do not want to be beaten. No, we refuse to be beaten!

One feature of the history of old Russia was the continual beatings she suffered because of her backwardness. She was beaten by the Mongol khans. She was beaten by the Turkish beys. She was beaten by the Swedish feudal lords. She was beaten by the Polish and Lithuanian gentry. She was beaten by the British and French capitalists. She was beaten by the Japanese barons. All beat her because of her backwardness, military backwardness, cultural backwardness, political backwardness, industrial backwardness, agricultural backwardness. They beat her because to do so was profitable and could be done with impunity.

Do you remember the words of the pre-Revolutionary poet: 'You are poor and abundant, mighty and impotent, Mother Russia.' Those gentlemen were quite familiar with the verses of the old poet. They beat her, saying: 'You are abundant; so one can enrich oneself at your expense.' They beat her, saying: 'You are poor and impotent, so you can be beaten and plundered with impunity.'

Such is the law of the exploiters - to beat the backward and the weak. It is the jungle law of capitalism. You are backward, you are weak - therefore you are wrong; hence, you can be beaten and enslaved. You are mighty - therefore you are right; hence, we must be wary of you...We are fifty or a hundred years behind the advanced countries. We must make good this distance in ten years. Either we do it, or we shall be crushed."[15]

This passage shows how when we are dominated by fear we lose all sense of the natural flow of human evolution. It tells us something about Stalin too: if we substitute the word 'Russia' in the speech for 'me', we gain an insight into his life experiences and attitudes. Rarely has the personal become so political.

---

[15] Joseph Stalin *On the Industrialisation of Russia* (Speech to industrial managers, February 1931)

In the end it is hard to say whether the old Tsarist regime or the new communist government brought greater suffering to the peoples of Russia. There was positive change – in education and social mobility for instance - in the new USSR but at a hideous price. It could take generations to heal the damage.

WOMEN'S RIVERLUTION

The story of the overthrow of the Tsarist regime also sheds light on an imbalance in the course of riverlution in human history: the inequality between the opportunities open to men to fulfil their potential compared to the endless restrictions placed on women.

In every area of life – the arts, science, industry, politics, leadership - above all in spirituality[16] – women have been held back from their natural evolution. Those who dared 'step out of line' - in reality claim their rightful place in the sun - were often subject to vicious punishments. There is a long and miserable list of lives lost, of talent thwarted, of souls suppressed: women's lives that could have been so much more but for fear, hatred and ignorance.

---

[16] The issue of women and spirituality is discussed in *Finding Jesus Ourselves* (Simenon Honoré, Spirit of the Rainbow, 2014)

One example is in the way male-female couples are treated differently. In Tsarist Russia, all power lay with Nicholas II. His wife, Alexandra, constitutionally had little or no authority. Her influence extended only as far as her husband might choose to listen to her or whatever powers he decided to temporarily delegate to her. Yet he has come down in popular history as nice but weak: she as strong and nasty. One standard history of Russia compared the royal pair:

> *"The empress, the reactionary, hysterical, and willful German princess Alexandra, became the power behind the throne...A good man, but a miserable ruler lost in the moment of crisis – no wonder Nicholas II has often been compared to Louis XVI."* [17]

The truth is they both held reactionary views but Nicholas alone was responsible for putting them into practice, whether it was deciding to shoot unarmed demonstrators, block parliamentary progress or encourage anti-Semitic pogroms. Yet in case any reader might have somehow missed his message, a few pages on the author repeated his judgement on her:

> *"A narrow-minded, reactionary, hysterical woman..."*

---

[17] Nicholas Riasanovsky *A History of Russia* (Oxford University Press, New York, 1977)

The choice of the word 'willful'[18] is revealing. It is usually used about children who won't do what they're told and maybe subconsciously that was the point the historian was trying to make. She 'didn't know her place' as a meek and humble wife and mother. In reality the only equality she ever achieved was in death when she was butchered in a cellar along with her husband and children in 1918.

Nor was this a one-off. The passage draws a parallel between the Tsar Nicholas II and Louis XVI of France that holds a truth though not in the sense it was meant: Louis XVI's wife, Queen Marie Antoinette, met with an almost identical response to Alexandra. Both when she was alive and in posterity, she was largely blamed for the failings of the regime even though she, like Alexandra, had no constitutional power. She became known as the 'Autrichienne'- a play on words coming from the fact she was Austrian but also carrying the double meaning of 'chienne' – a female dog or bitch: to her contemporaries, 'L'Autrichienne' came to mean 'the 'Austrian bitch'.[19]

These examples are only one tiny part of what may be called 'the war on women' – that is the widespread and

---

[18] American spelling
[19] Conor Byrne "The German Bitch": Alexandra Feodorovna, Marie Antoinette, and the Evil Foreign Queen in European Monarchy (University of St Andrews Historical Society, April 2014)

systematic repression of women and all they stood for that has lasted for centuries and that has stood the way of women's riverlution. Only now are we starting to take steps to redress a terrible historical wrong. Not only has it been a great injustice that has held women back; it has stifled a spirit in all of us, male and female; and it has damaged and distorted the natural development of all humanity.

ILLUMINATI AND PROUD

A number of conspiracy theories have swirled around the 1917 Russian Revolution. They raise a more general issue about the effect that conspiracies – real and imagined – have had on our human evolution.

For this reason it is important that we look at these claims with a well-informed and intelligent awareness. It has been claimed that the Russian Revolution came from nowhere and was in fact the result of a Masonic and/or Jewish plot. The first part of the claim is demonstrably untrue and the second is simply a gross misrepresentation of facts.

To take the first part: there was an attempted revolution in 1905 headed off by a mixture of government concessions and brute force; for a while the revolutionary tide subsided but it started to pick up again and by the eve of World War I it was on the rise.

A mountain of documents – police reports, ministerial papers and so on – provide evidence of a growing anxiety about the possibility of another revolution. The only significant figures who did not believe there would be a revolution were those distanced from the reality of Russian life such as Lenin, the Communist leader, in exile in Switzerland; and the Tsar cocooned in his own Imperial fantasy world. Pretty much everyone else knew. The Russian revolution was primarily the result of a government trying to block the natural flow of human development and was decades in the making.

The issue of Masonic involvement in the overthrow of the Tsar rests on the fact that some members of the Liberal opposition were Free Masons. But there was nothing sinister about it. In those days Free Masons acted as informal networks for reform-minded individuals and consequently were viewed with great suspicion by the government. Liberal Free Masons wanted constitutional reform, not the overthrow of the government: they were one manifestation of the natural riverlutionary flow that offered peaceful change.

In addition, at the turn of the 20th century all political opposition was outlawed in Russia and groups had to operate in secret: the Liberals were no exception. When they were legalised after 1905 the Liberals campaigned openly for change in Russia. Though they were very reluctant revolutionaries, they took part in the events of

1917. After the Tsar fell, some became members of a short-lived Provisional Government. All these facts are, and always were, in the public domain. But the revolution itself began as a spontaneous bread riot caused by food shortages in the midst of a war. There was no 'Masonic plot' just a desire for food and justice.

The 'Jewish Conspiracy' theory has two roots: the 'Protocols of the Elders of Zion', a well known Tsarist forgery designed to stir up hatred against Jews; and the fact that some Communists were Jewish, Trotsky being the most famous. It is wholly unsurprising that Jews, like other persecuted minorities in Russia, were to be found in opposition groups. They had little reason to support the Tsarist system that denied them their civil rights. The Communists, like other political groups, had to operate underground till they were briefly legalised in 1905. There was no 'Jewish plot' just the opposition of the oppressed. It is a natural part of our evolution for all humans to seek their rightful place in the sun.

But the idea of some shadowy organisation working with evil intent has deep roots in European culture: in the Middle Ages many people believed that there was a Jewish-Moslem-leper conspiracy to poison the wells and spread the Black Death. Christopher Marlowe draws on this myth in his play, the Jew of Malta (1584) when Barabas, a Jew, plots with Ithamore, a Moslem:

"As of thy fellow; we are villains both;
Both circumcised; we hate Christians both:
Be true and secret; thou shalt want no gold."

These conspiracy theories took on a new twist when secret societies sprang up during the 18th century Enlightenment to spread rationalist and reforming ideas and thus challenged the traditional power and influence of the Church and the state. As well as the Free Masons, a new society - the Illuminati – was set up by a Bavarian professor Adam Weishaupt in 1776. He saw a universal democratic republic where:

"...man will recover from his fall; princes and nations,
without violence to force them, will vanish from the
earth; the human race will become one family, and the
world the habitation of rational beings."[20]

Such a vision of society put them on a collision course with the authorities and the Duke of Bavaria outlawed the Illuminati and banished Weishaupt from his country in 1784. Similarly the Catholic Church under Pope Pius VI condemned the order the following year – a fact that doesn't seem to have deterred conspiracy theorists from seeing the Illuminati as a sinister element

---

[20] Adam Weishaupt *Die Lampe von Diogenese* (Translated Amelia Gill, The Masonic Book Club, 2008)

in the Catholic hierarchy. Much has been made of their secrecy but as U.S. President Thomas Jefferson wrote:[21]

> *"As Weishaupt lived under the tyranny of a despot and priests, he knew that caution was necessary even in spreading information, and the principles of pure morality...This has given an air of mystery to his views, was the foundation of his banishment...If Weishaupt had written here, where no secrecy is necessary in our endeavours to render men wise and virtuous, he would not have thought of any secret machinery for that purpose."*

Once the organisation had been driven underground people were free to speculate wildly on the extent of its influence or what its activities were. It certainly contained prominent members from the professional and upper classes.

The Illuminati's radical ideas were one expression of our search for human riverlution. They were shared with a wide range of Enlightenment thinkers, and came to bear fruit in the American and French Revolutions. Adam Weishaupt's prospect of a new world of "universal happiness, in a state of liberty and moral equality" has echoes to be found in the American Declaration of Independence in 1776:[22]

---

[21] Thomas Jefferson *Letters* (1800)
[22] See Chapter I

"We hold these truths to be self-evident: that all men are created equal; that they are endowed by their Creator with certain inalienable rights, that among them are life, liberty and the pursuit of happiness."

Similarities could also be found with the French Revolution's slogan of 'Liberty, Equality, Brotherhood'. This has been taken as proof that somehow the Illuminati orchestrated these events (quite a feat in the case of America as their Declaration of Independence was written within weeks of the founding of Weishaupt's group of only five members). The simple explanation is that the French and American revolutionaries together with the Illuminati (and many Free Masons) all drew on Enlightenment ideas. The riverlution of ideas has worked in this way throughout history: the moment comes when humanity needs to take a step forward and a new idea will manifest and spread outwards across many countries and groups. This is not a conspiracy: this is riverlution in action.

Real conspiracies exist: and it is certainly true that conspiracies, by their nature, work in secret; and some Masonic Lodges seem to have become more interested in power and wealth than their original liberal and humanitarian ideals as in the infamous P2 case in Italy. In 1981 a secret document was uncovered by the police listing leading members of the Italian political establishment, the armed forces, businessmen and newspaper editors as members of the P2 (Propaganda Two) Masonic Lodge. The Prime Minister had to resign amidst claims that the P2 Masonic Lodge was running 'a state within a state'.

Key to uncovering conspiracies like this is a free press, an honest police force and an independent judiciary. This is what we need to focus on: making sure we have the will and the means to expose wrongdoing and holding those responsible to account. This is what will enable humanity to evolve freely.

Cases like P2 are serious but they should not be used to create false narratives based on medieval prejudices. The Illuminati took their name from the 'illuminating' grace of Christ and originally did not allow Jews or pagans to join. Nevertheless the old anti-Semitic myths became intertwined with dark suspicions about this and other secret societies to balloon into a fantasy of a world-wide Jewish-Illuminati-Masonic conspiracy.

Wallowing in world of fear and paranoia, constructing imaginary global conspiracies does no-one any good. It creates a negative victim mentality when we need to be empowering ourselves to work positively for the well-being of humanity and the planet. The power of riverlution, of the evolutionary flow of the universe, of the inevitability of good, is irresistible. Any conspiracy can only delay human evolution: it cannot stop it or significantly divert its path. In the end, conspiracies are simply irrelevant.

As for the Illuminati, their overall objective was "the happiness of the human race"; they promoted women's education and equality; they worked to free human enquiry from the stifling authority of the Church and state; they concerned themselves with the suffering of the poor and opposed the rigid class hierarchy of 18th century society. For them, "illumination" meant "enlightening the understanding by the sun of reason which will dispel the clouds of superstition and prejudice."[23] The need to work in secret does not necessarily mean having a malevolent purpose.

The reality is that the Illuminati were one of a number of groups that can be traced through history working to spread the light of universal humanity and spirituality. These groups are there to inspire and encourage the peoples of this planet forward in our evolution. If working - whether in secret or in the open - for a world where we can live as one people in harmony, freedom and equality makes me part of a global conspiracy then I am proud to call myself an Illuminati.

---

[23] Adam Weishaupt *Sidonii Apollinarus Fragment* (Germany, 1774)

CHAPTER IV

Planetary Riverlution

In 1915 the geophysicist Alfred Lothar Wegener coined the term 'Pangaea'[24] to describe a supercontinent that existed 250 million years ago. The seven continents on which we live were once united in this single great landmass. These drifted apart over hundreds of millions of years to form our present continents of Africa, Asia, Australasia, Europe and the Americas.

They are now in the process of slowly coming together again: so the Mediterranean will gradually disappear as Africa moves towards southern Europe; and geologists estimate that about 250 million years from now there will be a new supercontinent, called variously 'Novopangaea', 'Amasia' and 'Pangaea Ultima' – the last a somewhat misleading name as far from being the ultimate landmass, in time it will break apart like all the other supercontinents. In the hundred years since Wegener's discovery scientists have come to believe that the process of continents breaking up and coming together again in new forms - the Supercontinent Cycle

---

[24] Alfred Lothar Wegener *The Origins of Continents and Oceans* (Geologische Rundschau, Germany, 1864)

- has happened many times before and will happen many times again. [25]

This flow of continents outwards from a single landmass that in turn return to a new supercontinent has echoes with the Big Crunch and cyclical theories of the universe as well as the journey of the soul. Such a flow is the hallmark of riverlution.

LEMURIA AND ATLANTIS

This is not the only parallel between the formation of continents and the cosmos. There is the same interplay between the intellect and the intuition in the theories about their development.

Pangaea itself – the supercontinent where dinosaurs once roamed – was itself formed of two enormous landmasses joined near the Equator. In the north was Laurasia -North America, Europe and much of Asia - and in the south lay Gondwanaland – South America, Africa, India, Australasia and Antarctica.

The break up of Pangaea – the riverlutionary flow of continents outwards - was to have an effect on the development and distribution of different species of

[25] I am deeply indebted in this chapter for the work of the writer and geologist Dr Ted Nield in his fascinating and detailed account of the evolution of continents from his book *Supercontinent* (Granta, London, 2007)

plants and animals on the planet and at first it created some puzzles. In particular scientists were trying to discover why similar species existed in areas separated by vast distances of water. This in turn gave rise to two controversial theories – Atlantis and Lemuria.

In 1864 the biogeographer Philip Sclater published an article on the distribution of Lemurs and their close relatives. [26] These primates are to be found off the coast of Africa on the island of Madagascar and also in southern India and Sri Lanka. Sclater offered an explanation and fatefully gave a name to a 'lost continent'[27]:

"A large continent occupied parts of the Atlantic and Indian Oceans...that this continent was broken up into islands, of which some have become amalgamated with...Africa, some...with what is now Asia; and that in Madagascar and the Mascarene Islands we have the existing relics of this great continent, for which...I should propose the name **Lemuria***!*

The idea of a lost continent was taken up by the psychic and founder of the new religion of Theosophy, Madame Blavatsky. In *The Secret Doctrine*[28] she

---

[26] Philip Sclater The Mammals of Madagascar (*Quarterly Journal of Science*, 1864)

[27] Quoted by Dr Ted Nield *Supercontinent* (Granta, London, 2007)

[28] Madame Blavatsky *The Secret Doctrine* (Theosophical University Press, 1888)

55

explained how the inhabitants of our planet evolved through a number of root races, of which the third lived on the continent of Lemuria. These Lemurians were immensely tall compared to modern humans, "highly intelligent"[29] with strongly developed psychic abilities. Co-existing with dinosaurs, in their earlier history they laid eggs but later evolved mammalian reproduction.

The controversy over Lemuria took a further twist when it became intertwined with the ancient Tamil story of Kumarikkantam. The Tamils, who speak a language older than Sanskrit, live in eastern and southern India and also Sri Lanka. Their literature speaks of a catastrophic flood that sunk much of what was once their homeland.

Unsurprisingly, Sclater's theories seem to provide geological proof of the legend. Unhappily this marriage between modern science and ancient myth was not to last as geologists began to explain the puzzle of the Lemurs *solely* by the moving apart of landmasses from old Gondwanaland into the modern continents of Africa and Asia. However with continuing deep sea exploration in the Indian Ocean the final chapter on Lemuria may not yet be closed.

The break-up of Pangaea was to give rise to another controversy: Atlantis. As with the story of Lemuria, it

---

[29] Ibid

began with the issue of finding similarities between plants, animals and even human culture separated by wide oceans this time on either side of the Atlantic. Yet another island seemed to offer an answer: Atlantis.[30] The earliest record of its existence takes us back to Plato's writings.[31] Whether he meant it as history or allegory, [32] he clearly placed it in the Atlantic as shown by his description:

> *"These histories tell of a mighty power which was aggressing wantonly against the whole of Europe and Asia[33]...This power came forth out of the Atlantic Ocean, for in those days the Atlantic was navigable; and there was an island situated in front of the straits which you call the Columns of Hercules: [34] the island larger than Libya and Asia put together, and this was the way to other islands, and from the islands you might pass through the whole of the opposite continent which surrounded the true ocean; for this sea which is within the Straits of Hercules is only a harbour, having a narrow entrance..."*

---

[30] According to Madame Blavatsky the inhabitants of Atlantis were the 4th root race; humans are the 5th.

[31] Plato (c.424 – 348 BCE) *Timaeus* (c.360 BCE, Greece)

[32] In *Timaeus* the story is described as "not as a mere legend but a veritable action of the Athenian state".

[33] By 'Asia' he would have been referring to the area roughly covering what is now called the Middle East.

[34] This was the ancient Greek name for the Straits of Gibraltar - the entrance to the Mediterranean Sea. Mountainous headlands in Greece had been given this name but other elements of his story place it at the Straits of Gibraltar.

Despite this clear signposting, any number of historians and geologists have tried to explain this story by claiming it referred to the island of Thera off the Greek coast that suffered a cataclysmic volcanic eruption c.1600 BCE and sunk.[35] Additionally the layout of Atlantis with its concentric canals is quite unlike anything discovered by archaeologists in Thera or the islands nearby. Whether we believe Plato's story or not, it was definitely meant to be in the Atlantic.

Plato's story might have remained simply a curiosity, the preserve of scholars of the ancient world. But 19th century biogeographers who faced a similar problem to Sclater in explaining similarities between species on either side of the Atlantic, opened up the possibility that the 'legend' of Atlantis might just provide a solution. In 1882 this idea became known to the wider public with Ignatius Donnelly's *Atlantis The Antediluvian World*,[36] which laid out in great detail the evidence for there having been a land bridge between Africa, Europe and America.

But in the absence (yet) of any physical evidence of a sunken island this theory was eventually discarded, like that about Lemuria. Instead scientists came to

---

[35] Thera may have another significance: some Biblical scholars argue the eruption may have been a key event in the Exodus from Egypt – see also Simenon Honoré *Walking With Moses* (Spirit of the Rainbow, UK, 2016)
[36] Ignatius Donnelly's *Atlantis The Antediluvian World* (Harper & Brothers, New York, 1882)

believe that the break-up of Gondwanaland that once united Africa and South America was the only reason for the biological and cultural similarities both sides of the Atlantic. There was the reassuring evidence that the eastern coast of South America fitted snugly into the western shoreline of Africa. This riverlutionary pulling apart of continents seemed to have a simple solution.

But Donnelley's map places Atlantis quite far north, west of the Azores in the mid Atlantic and so could be consistent with the splitting apart of Gondwanaland into the continents of Africa and South America. There is plenty of evidence of large islands being destroyed by natural disasters so it would be wise not to shut the book on Atlantis too hastily.

THE MYSTERY OF URANTIA

It would be particularly wise in light of the strange story found in *The Urantia Book*. Published in 1934, these spiritual writings were said to come from a 'Higher Source'. 'Urantia' was the name given to our planet whose evolution it described from the earliest moments of its creation. At a time when geologists believed Pangaea was the original supercontinent, the book described a supercontinent *before* Pangaea: [37]

---

[37] *The Urantia Book* - Part III. The History Of Urantia Paper 57: Section 8 (Urantia Foundation, USA)

"1,000,000,000 years ago is the date of the actual beginning of Urantia history...At the opening of this faraway era, Urantia should be envisaged as a water-bound planet. Later on, deeper and hence denser lava flows came out upon the bottom of the present Pacific Ocean, and this part of the water-covered surface became considerably depressed. The first continental land mass emerged from the world ocean...

950,000,000 years ago Urantia presents the picture of one great continent of land and one large body of water, the Pacific Ocean. Volcanoes are still widespread and earthquakes are both frequent and severe.

The Urantia Book then described its break-up:

"750,000,000 years ago the first breaks in the continental land mass began..."

The book went on to explain that these new landmasses in turn gave rise to shallow ocean basins in which early life could develop:

"...the further separation of the landmasses and, in consequence, a further extension of the continental seas ... these inland seas of olden times were truly the cradle of evolution."

At the time it is doubtful if any professional geologist was aware of these writings and, if they had been, they would hardly have taken them seriously.

It was not until 1970 that two geologists James W. Valentine and Eldridge M. Moores published a paper suggesting that earlier supercontinents existed. It would mean that the flow of continents breaking apart and then coming together to form a new supercontinent was cyclical. And it echoed theories of our universe.

Further work by Professor Mark McMenamin established the geological evidence for a supercontinent and gave the landmass its name of Rodinia (taken from the Russian word for birthplace).[38]

And he dated it: *one billion years old* – the same date as *The Urantia Book*. His description followed a similar pattern of continental break-up and its importance in creating the conditions for early life as *The Urantia Book*.

In a later work,[39] Mark McMenamin wrote about the parallels between his discoveries and the section in *The Urantia Book* about the supercontinent and the role its break-up played in creating conditions for early life:

---

[38] Mark & Dianna McMenamin *The Emergence of Animals: the Cambrian Breakthrough* (Columbia University Press, 1990)

[39] Mark McMenamin *The Garden of Ediacara: Discovering the First Complex Life* (Columbia University Press, New York, 1998)

"This amazing passage, written in the 1930s, anticipates scientific results that did not actually appear in the scientific literature until many decades later."

He added cautiously:

"Of course I am being selective here in my choice of quotations, and there are reams of scientifically untenable material in The Urantia Book."

The Urantia Book and Mark McMenamin's comments are important in several ways: first – unlike Madame Blavatsky and Ignatius Donnelly – this mystical work revealed a supercontinent and thus a cyclical evolution of landmasses before the scientific community was even aware of its existence.

Second, intuition is only as good an instrument as its user: some of what was written in *The Urantia Book* may be off the mark or impossible to prove or disprove: that does not take away from its accuracy in seeing key steps of our planet's evolution.

Finally, it is entirely to Mark McMenamin's credit that he was opened-minded enough to publicly acknowledge the parallels between *The Urantia Book* and his own geological research. Furthermore, he went on to suggest it could be worthwhile for scientists to study other mystical writings.[40]

This interaction between the intellect and intuition forms one of the recurring themes in our exploration of riverlution.

The development of supercontinents is also part of a wider picture of evolution that our planet is going through, whatever the debates over its details. And thus in turn it becomes part of our great story of riverlution.

---

[40] Mark McMenamin *The Garden of Ediacara: Discovering the First Complex Life* (Columbia University Press, New York, 1998)

CONCLUSION

Towards A Spiritual Riverlution

Riverlution – the universal flow of evolution – is inevitable and irresistible. The issue is what we choose to do about it. Do we choose to go with the spiritual flow of our lives and seek out our highest destiny? Or do we choose to resist the flow, living a half-life in the shadows, never becoming the person we could?

Within our inner world lies the story of our evolution: we find our reptilian psyche, focused on survival with little or no feeling; our mammalian psyche, with a greater capacity for feeling and focused on power, hierarchy and territory; and our human psyche, opening to a wider world where we sense our connection to the whole universe; where our natural curiosity urges us to experience and explore; where we become self-aware, asking ourselves questions about our existence.

Every one of us will experience all these levels of consciousness at one time or another in our lives. Which level we choose to live at is the issue. In our prayers, in our meditation, in our stillness we can sense the flow of our spiritual evolution and make the decision to go with it. The changes in our lives may come slowly, they may come fast, but they will come.

When we allow ourselves to follow the sacred river, it will grow ever stronger inside us. We will feel its irresistible flow direct our lives more clearly. And as we surrender to its Divine current we become one with our Creator. That is the promise of riverlution.

THE LIGHTS OF RIVERLUTION

We are not alone. Our path is illuminated by great souls that have come to show us that it can be done – that if we surrender to the flow our highest destiny awaits.

One is Dr Martin Luther King. The work he did was not just for African Americans or civil rights or even for all of the United States of America: it was for humanity. He was in the true sense, a prophet. He lived that sense of riverlution, of the natural and peaceful change that human evolution involves. He saw beyond his moment in history. He said so quite clearly:

> *"Like anybody, I would like to live a long life. Longevity has its place. But I'm not concerned about that now. I just want to do God's will. And He's allowed me to go up to the mountain. And I've looked over. And I've seen the Promised Land. I may not get there with you. But I want you to know tonight, that we, as a people, will get to the Promised Land!*

And so I'm happy, tonight.

I'm not worried about anything.

I'm not fearing any man!

Mine eyes have seen the glory of the coming of the Lord!!"[41]

Hours later Martin Luther King was dead. That fact may have deflected people from actually hearing what he was saying and really thinking about it:

"And I've looked over. And I've seen the Promised Land."

What an astonishing claim! In a heightened spiritual state, he was able to go beyond our normal horizon and see into our future. In so doing he affirmed the irresistible flow of our human evolution and the inevitability of goodness.

This is the message of riverlution.

---

[41] Martin Luther King *I've Been To The Mountaintop* (Speech at Mason Temple Church of God in Christ Headquarters, Memphis, Tennessee, 3 April 1968)

BOOKS BY SIMENON HONORÉ

WE ARE ONE *A Manifesto for Humanity*

"Great book expressing our common humanity.
Congratulations Simenon."
PETER TATCHELL, Human Rights Activist

"What can I say? Your manuscript was simply marvelous. There were countless times when I held my breath, shook my head, shouted 'Amen!' and even had to just place my laptop down and contemplate."
ESTARI LAMAR POWERS, Poet and Activist

"A call to action, a rallying cry and I felt motivated to see how I could do more to bring this unity into consciousness."
MATTHEW CLARKE, Artist, Musician & Film Maker

We Are One: *A Manifesto for Humanity* offers a practical vision of a society based on the interconnectedness of all life. From the atoms that make up all existence on earth to the atomic bomb that threatens to destroy it, our fates are indissolubly bound together. It is this that holds the key to resolving the issues that confront us both as individuals and as a planet. It is this too that empowers us to build a better future for ourselves and our precious earth.

We Are One provides ideas for a programme of personal and planetary change. Topics include:

- **9/11: A CHANCE FOR WORLD HEALING**
- **A COUNTRY CALLED EARTH**
- **JUSTICE WITHOUT PUNISHMENT**
- **RESPECT AND REVERENCE FOR ALL LIFE**
- **WE HAVE THE POWER TO CHANGE THE WORLD**

We Are One is a book that gives hope to the world.

WELCOME TO PLANET EARTH
A Guide For Awakening Souls

"Welcome to Planet Earth is an operating manual for this often complex 'inner organism' of who we are, which we all need to learn how to navigate; the ways and means for more balance and joy in our life through deeper self-knowledge."

PATRICK HOUSER, *Author and Educator*

"I read this book avidly from start to finish. It feels strongly spiritual and the author has had his own experiences of enlightenment."

CELIA GAIL STUART, *Healer & Psychic Counsellor*

"It explores a whole new way of looking at the problems we face right now and an invigorating one. It makes a refreshing change. A very fine addition to the We Are One Series."

ANN BARTER, *Spiritual Psychotherapist & Colour Healer*

Welcome To Planet Earth opens new horizons for readers starting on their spiritual exploration. Using both the intellect and intuition, and drawing on authentic life experiences, it offers insights into questions we may ask ourselves as we awaken to our soul's calling:

- WHO AM I?
- WHAT AM I DOING HERE ON EARTH?
- WHAT IS MY SOUL PURPOSE?
- HOW DO I FREE MY SOUL?

"Whatever task our soul has been given we will have also been provided with the inner resources to do it. We are not being given an impossible task any more than we are given nothing to do. During the course of our lives the balance between challenge and support may change; at times it may feel too much; but we begin life with all the tools we need to fulfil our soul purpose."

FINDING JESUS OURSELVES
A Path of Spiritual Empowerment

This book strips away the centuries of dogma and Church teaching about Jesus and takes us back to the drawing board so we can begin our own authentic quest. Using both the intellect and intuition, it takes us through some of the question about Jesus:

- Where do our ideas about Jesus come from?

- Who or what should we trust to guide us?

- How can we create our own path to Jesus?

Christianity has often focused on us believing the 'right' things:

"Historically Church doctrine has hung on to its own certainties wherever it can. What is more it has clung resolutely to doctrines whose importance to real life is mystifying. Take for example the doctrine of Virgin Birth. It is a piece of dogma over which not only a great deal of ink has been spilt but regrettably a great deal of blood too. There are two basic questions we could ask about this doctrine:

Who knows? Who cares?"

Finding Jesus Ourselves challenges the Church's role as the 'shepherd' of our soul. As earlier Gnostic writings pointed out:

"They did not realise that she has an invisible spiritual body, thinking, "We are her shepherd who feeds her." But they did not realise that she knows another way, which is hidden from them…"

The way is open for us to create our own path to Jesus by embracing the 'female', 'male' and 'child' parts of our spirituality.

Finding Jesus Ourselves is a book that supports us in making our own choices as we explore our spirituality.

THE COMMUNITY OF CHRIST

The Community of Christ opens a new horizon for us in seeing Jesus' mission as delivering a Universal message for humanity not limited to any one religious doctrine. By using both the intellect and intuition, it enables the reader to explore the different understandings of Jesus: the man, the Messenger, the 'Son of God'.

The book looks afresh at Jesus' mission on earth and questions whether his purpose really was his death as a means of salvation for humanity. Rather his work was to bring new life to this planet by his very presence.

"It was his life that was at the heart of the message he had for humanity. He was so alive, more alive than any other human being, he shone with it. If his ministry has a central point, it is the Sermon on the Mount. For there he was as the morning sun. His very being was filled with such a light that it radiated across the world: subtly, invisibly, yet with unimaginable power...There was his message to humanity. There the seeds of the Kingdom of Heaven on earth were planted."

The book presents a vision of the re-unification of Christianity bypassing the traditional institutions and bringing together its Jewish, Gnostic and orthodox roots into a Universal message.

The community of Christ has no boundaries. In the end everyone belongs because in the end everyone is part of God and is drawn to their Creator, however many lifetimes it takes. They will be those who follow Christ in their daily lives, whatever name they give to their beliefs. For others there will be a searching out, a questioning, a sense of unease that indicates the first stirrings of a spiritual awakening however painful and slow it may feel. Then there are those locked in the realm of their shadows, slaves to their fear, their addictions and their sense of separation. Still even here a light shines, perhaps beyond consciousness yet growing towards that first moment of illumination. All are within the community of Christ.

70

COMING OUT IN SPRING 2015:

EDUCATION FOR HUMANITY

Based on spiritual insights and more than a quarter of a century's experience in the classroom, this book asks the question:

WHAT IS EDUCATION FOR?

Its answer is as simple as it is radical: the development of fully human beings. The book provides not only the thinking behind its ideas but also practical solutions based on case studies.

Central to its message is that the only way we develop morally and spiritually is by example and that teachers can support students, not by being saints but by being human: doing their best, not being afraid to admit mistakes, allowing for the ups and downs of life.

Education for Humanity a visionary book grounded in the reality of 21st century education.

≈

COMING OUT IN SPRING 2016:

WALKING WITH MOSES:
Journey to the Promised Land

This is the first volume of a spiritual autobiography that takes the story of Moses and the Exodus as its central theme both as part of our inheritance and moral lesson for our times. It weaves itself into the author's own struggle for freedom from his inner slavery – a struggle that takes him from Israel to Mongolia in his search for the 'Promised Land'. *Walking with Moses* is not just a story about one individual or one historical event: it is a story for all humanity.

71